MULTIPLE SKILLS SERIES: Reading

Third Edition

Richard A. Boning

Columbus, Ohio

A Division of The McGraw-Hill Companies

Cover, Charlie Waite/Tony Stone Images

SRA/McGraw-Hill

A Division of The ***McGraw-Hill*** *Companies*

Printed in the United States of America.

Send all inquiries to:
SRA/McGraw-Hill
250 Old Wilson Bridge Road
Suite 310
Worthington, Ohio 43085

ISBN 0-02-688420-8

4 5 6 7 8 9 SCG 02 01 00 99

To the Teacher

PURPOSE

The ***Multiple Skills Series*** is a nonconsumable reading program designed to develop a cluster of key reading skills and to integrate these skills with each other and with the other language arts. ***Multiple Skills*** is also diagnostic, making it possible for you to identify specific types of reading skills that might be causing difficulty for individual students.

FOR WHOM

The twelve levels of the ***Multiple Skills Series*** are geared to students who comprehend on the pre-first- through ninth-grade reading levels.

- The Picture Level is for children who have not acquired a basic sight vocabulary.
- The Preparatory 1 Level is for children who have developed a limited basic sight vocabulary.
- The Preparatory 2 Level is for children who have a basic sight vocabulary but are not yet reading on the first-grade level.
- Books A through I are appropriate for students who can read on grade levels one through nine respectively. Because of their high interest level, the books may also be used effectively with students functioning at these levels of competence in other grades.

The **Multiple Skills Series Placement Tests** will help you determine the appropriate level for each student.

PLACEMENT TESTS

The Elementary Placement Test (for grades Pre-1 through 3) and the Midway Placement Tests (for grades 4–9) will help you place each student properly. The tests consist of representative units selected from the series. The test books contain two forms, X and Y. One form may be used for placement and the second as a posttest to measure progress. The tests are easy to administer and score. Blackline Masters are provided for worksheets and student performance profiles.

THE BOOKS

This third edition of the ***Multiple Skills Series*** maintains the quality and focus that have distinguished this program for over 25 years. The series includes four books at each level, Picture Level through Level I. Each book in the Picture Level through Level B contains 25 units. Each book in Level C through Level I contains 50 units. The units within each book increase in difficulty. The books within a level also increase in difficulty—Level A, Book 2 is slightly more difficult than Level A, Book 1, and so on. This gradual increase in difficulty permits students to advance from one book to the next and from one level to the next without frustration.

Each book contains an **About This Book** page, which explains the skills to the students and shows them how to approach reading the selections and questions. In the lowest levels, you should read About This Book to the children.

The questions that follow each unit are designed to develop specific reading skills. In the lowest levels, you should read the questions to the children. In Level C, the question pattern in each unit is

1. Title (main idea)
2. Stated detail
3. Stated detail
4. Inference or conclusion
5. Vocabulary

The **Language Activity Pages** (LAP) in each level consist of four parts: Exercising Your Skill, Expanding Your Skill, Exploring Language, and Expressing Yourself. These pages lead the students beyond the book through a broadening spiral of writing, speaking, and other individual and group language activities that apply, extend, and integrate the skills being developed. You may use all, some, or none of the activities in any LAP; however, some LAP activities depend on preceding ones. In the lowest levels, you should read the LAPs to the children.

In Levels C-I, each set of Language Activity Pages focuses on a particular skill developed through the book. Emphasis progresses from the most concrete to the most abstract:

First LAP	Details
Second LAP	Vocabulary
Third LAP	Main ideas
Last LAP	Inferences and conclusions

SESSIONS

The ***Multiple Skills Series*** is an individualized reading program that may be used with small groups or an entire class. Short sessions are the most effective. Use a short session every day or every other day, completing a few units in each session. Time allocated to the Language Activity Pages depends on the abilities of the individual students.

SCORING

Students should record their answers on the reproducible worksheets. The worksheets make scoring easier and provide uniform records of the children's work. Using worksheets also avoids consuming the books.

Because it is important for the students to know how they are progressing, you should score the units as soon as they've been completed. Then you can discuss the questions and activities with the students and encourage them to justify their responses. Many of the LAPs are open-ended and do not lend themselves to an objective score; for this reason, there are no answer keys for these pages.

About This Book

A careful reader thinks about the writer's words and pays attention to what the story or article is mainly about. A careful reader also "reads between the lines" because a writer does not tell the reader everything. A careful reader tries to figure out the meaning of new words too. As you read the stories and articles in this book, you will practice all of these reading skills.

First you will read a story and choose a good title for it. The title will tell something about the **main idea** of the article or story. To choose a good title, you must know what the story or article is mainly about.

The next two questions will ask you about facts that are stated in the story or article. To answer these questions, read carefully. Pay attention to the **details.**

The fourth question will ask you to figure out **something the writer doesn't tell you directly.** For example, you might read that Dr. Fujihara received an emergency call, drove to Elm Street, and rushed into a house. Even though the writer doesn't tell you directly, you can figure out that Dr. Fujihara knows how to drive and that someone in the house is probably sick. You use the information the author provides plus your own knowledge and experience to figure out what is probably true.

The last question will ask you to tell the meaning of a word in the story or article. You can figure out what the word means by studying its **context**—the other words and sentences in the story. Read the following sentences.

> Ted pulled and pulled on the line. The big fish pulled too. After more than an hour, Ted was finally able to pull the fish out of the water. He had caught his first *salmon.*

Did you figure out that a salmon is a kind of fish? What clues in the story helped you figure this out?

This book will help you practice your reading skills. As you learn to use all of these skills together, you will become a better reader.

UNIT 1

More than anything else, Joan wanted to play in a band. Whenever a favorite song came on the radio, she would sing the words and pretend to play the guitar. "Some day," she told herself, "people will *applaud* when I sing."

Finally, she asked Marty Sanchez if she could see his band, The Express, practice. At first, Joan just watched quietly. Then she began humming and singing along during practices. Now she sings with them at dances and concerts. "I still can't play the guitar," she tells people, "but I am the main singer. In fact, we changed the name of the band to Joanie and The Express!"

---

1. The best title is—
   (A) People Who Like Music
   (B) Joan Joins a Band
   (C) The Express
   (D) Learning to Play

2. Joan pretended to play—
   (A) many instruments
   (B) with her own band
   (C) at a dance
   (D) the guitar

3. At first, Joan sang only—
   (A) at dances
   (B) on weekends
   (C) during practice
   (D) for her family

4. You can tell that Joan—
   (A) likes to dance
   (B) sings well
   (C) plays guitar
   (D) is Marty's sister

5. The word "applaud" in line four means—
   (A) clap
   (B) laugh
   (C) play
   (D) talk

UNIT 2

Not many five-year-old boys own a real automobile. Jimmy Conway did—until he sold it.

Jimmy's parents bought three tickets. The tickets were for chances to win a new car. They wrote Jimmy's name on one of the tickets. When the winning ticket was picked, it was Jimmy's. He had won a new automobile!

Jimmy couldn't drive the car because he was a *minor*. It would be many years before he would be old enough. So Jimmy sold his car. He was still happy because he was able to put lots of money in the bank.

---

1. The best title is—
   (A) Learning to Ride a Horse
   (B) A Boy Wins a Car
   (C) Going to the Bank
   (D) A Man Buys a Car

2. Jimmy Conway won—
   (A) an old automobile
   (B) a ticket
   (C) a job
   (D) a new automobile

3. The story says that Jimmy—
   (A) ate a lot
   (B) sold the car
   (C) fixed the car
   (D) hit the car

4. When Jimmy won the car, he was—
   (A) an old man
   (B) five years old
   (C) learning to drive
   (D) working in a bank

5. The word "minor" in line seven means—
   (A) doll
   (B) clown
   (C) child
   (D) grandfather

UNIT 3

Clocks and watches help us to get places on time. A *glimpse* at a watch and we know if we have to hurry or can take our time. But what about people who are blind? They can't see what time it is.

Blind people can use a "talking watch." The watch shows the correct time, but it also has a button. When the button is pressed, a voice "tells" the time. Even people who are not blind find the talking watch useful at night.

The talking watch is a great help to everyone.

---

1. The best title is—
   (A) Going on a Trip
   (B) Why People Hate Watches
   (C) A Person Who Fixes Watches
   (D) A Watch That Talks

2. For the talking watch to "tell" the time, you must—
   (A) press a button
   (B) shake it
   (C) sell it
   (D) pull a string

3. The story says that blind people cannot—
   (A) have friends
   (B) hear music
   (C) hear the time
   (D) see the time

4. For blind people to use the talking watch, they must use their—
   (A) feet
   (B) ears
   (C) eyes
   (D) back

5. The word "glimpse" in line one means—
   (A) smell
   (B) look
   (C) taste
   (D) hit

UNIT 4

Sandra has a job "baby-sitting." Every day she feeds her "babies," changes their diapers, and takes them to a playground. This may not seem like an unusual job, but it is, because Sandra's "babies" are chimps.

Sandra works at a school that studies chimps and apes. The school wants to find out all it can about the animals. Sandra's *responsibility* is to care for the chimps. She says that they are just like real children. They laugh, play, and sometimes even argue. Sandra loves her "baby-sitting" job. She also loves her "babies."

---

1. The best title is—
   (A) Fun at a Playground
   (B) Why Apes Are Dangerous
   (C) Taking Care of Chimps
   (D) How to Feed Babies

2. Sandra works at a school that—
   (A) teaches children
   (B) studies chimps
   (C) sells food
   (D) makes chairs

3. Every day Sandra—
   (A) gets hurt
   (B) hunts animals
   (C) reads stories
   (D) changes diapers

4. The chimps are like real children because they—
   (A) run away
   (B) study spelling
   (C) act like children
   (D) look like children

5. The word "responsibility" in line six means—
   (A) family
   (B) money
   (C) game
   (D) job

UNIT 5

Almost all Americans have heard of Disneyland—the famous amusement park in California. Although Disneyland is a wonderful amusement park, it was not the first in the world.

There is an amusement park in the country of Denmark that is more than a hundred years old. It is called Tivoli. Tivoli has twenty acres of rides, theaters, and restaurants.

The king of Denmark built this park in 1843 to keep the people of his country happy. Since Tivoli opened, more than one hundred and fifty million people have visited it. They all say that the king did a *splendid* job.

---

1. The best title is—
   (A) A Hospital in Denmark
   (B) Going to the Theater
   (C) An Amusement Park in Denmark
   (D) A New Park

2. The amusement park in Denmark is called—
   (A) King's Park
   (B) Happy Town
   (C) Disneyland
   (D) Tivoli

3. The story says that the park in Denmark has—
   (A) stores
   (B) barber shops
   (C) rides
   (D) lakes

4. People go to an amusement park to—
   (A) work
   (B) have fun
   (C) buy clothes
   (D) sleep

5. The word "splendid" in line ten means—
   (A) terrible
   (B) very good
   (C) simple
   (D) weak

UNIT 6

When James Stevens was a young boy, he was saved by a horse!

James was swimming when the current carried him seventy-five yards from land. He tried to swim to shore but the current was too strong. A police officer saw that James was in trouble. The officer *mounted* his horse. The horse ran into the water and swam through the waves to James. The police officer put a rope around the boy, and the horse pulled him to shore.

The current had been too strong for the officer to swim to James, but not for his horse. The horse had saved James Stevens' life.

---

1. The best title is—
   (A) Learning to Swim
   (B) Training Horses
   (C) Saved by a Horse
   (D) A Day at the Beach

2. The police officer saw that James was—
   (A) laughing (B) singing
   (C) building castles (D) in trouble

3. James was carried far from land by a—
   (A) boat (B) current
   (C) fish (D) sail

4. If the horse hadn't been able to swim, James might have—
   (A) been happier (B) grown older
   (C) drowned (D) learned to swim

5. The word "mounted" in line five means—
   (A) climbed on (B) sold
   (C) bought (D) cleaned

UNIT 7

Every day, Ann Jacobs spends her day talking with people. She talks in her office, at home, and in businesses all around the city. What keeps her so busy is Senior Service. Senior Service is a job *agency* for older people. Ann Jacobs started this company soon after she left her job with a phone company.

"Senior Service," she explains, "helps everyone. Groups and businesses always need part-time workers. Many older people love to work a few hours each week. Our people work everywhere, from day-care centers to auto repair shops. And," she says proudly, "our people are always some of the best workers."

---

1. The best title is—
   (A) Auto Repair Jobs
   (B) Ann Jacobs' Senior Service
   (C) Ann Jacobs of the Phone Company
   (D) Using the Telephone for Business

2. Ann Jacobs worked at—
   (A) City Hall
   (B) a day-care center
   (C) an auto repair shop
   (D) a phone company

3. Senior Service is for—
   (A) young and old
   (B) just men
   (C) older people
   (D) just women

4. You can tell that Ann Jacobs likes to work with—
   (A) cars
   (B) people
   (C) tools
   (D) children

5. The word "agency" in line four means—
   (A) club
   (B) company
   (C) store
   (D) school

UNIT 8

George Hill was thirteen when his father brought home eight locks he had found. He didn't have a key for any of them. As a joke, he told George that he would give him twenty-five cents for each lock he could open. In only one hour, George had opened them all!

That's when George first became interested in locks. He read every book he could find about locks, and bought locks of all kinds. Today, George has a *vast* collection of locks. It is the largest collection in the world.

---

1. The best title is—
   (A) How to Earn Money
   (B) George and His Locks
   (C) Be Sure to Lock Your Door
   (D) George Takes a Trip

2. George opened the eight locks in—
   (A) two days
   (B) one year
   (C) one hour
   (D) three weeks

3. George read every book he could find about—
   (A) money
   (B) locks
   (C) stamps
   (D) games

4. You can tell from the story that George can—
   (A) run very fast
   (B) fix bicycles
   (C) open locks without keys
   (D) cook his own food

5. The word "vast" in line seven means—
   (A) all paper
   (B) very large
   (C) small
   (D) cheap

UNIT 9

Maria always says she has one of the world's best jobs. She works for the National Park Service at the Statue of Liberty in New York City. "People come here from all over the world," Maria says. "Helping them learn about 'Lady Liberty' is really exciting."

Maria begins her day just like one of the visitors. She takes a fifteen-minute boat ride to Liberty Island, where the statue stands. Then she helps visitors see the *exhibits* in the museum. The museum is inside the famous statue. Maria often talks with visitors as they climb to the statue's crown. "It's fun to talk with all these people," she says. "Besides, it gives me my exercise. There are 154 steps on the way to that crown!"

---

1. The best title is—
   (A) Maria's Job
   (B) How the Statue of Liberty Was Built
   (C) National Parks
   (D) Maria

2. Maria gets to the Statue of Liberty by—
   (A) train (B) helicopter
   (C) car (D) boat

3. The Statue of Liberty is—
   (A) on Manhattan Island (B) 154 feet tall
   (C) on Liberty Island (D) in a museum

4. Maria gets plenty of exercise when she—
   (A) rides to work (B) climbs to the crown
   (C) plays baseball (D) leaves work

5. The word "exhibits" in line seven means—
   (A) people (B) things for sale
   (C) things being shown (D) stairs

UNIT 10

Your grandfather had to walk five miles in the snow to get to school. Your mother had to walk three miles in a thunderstorm to get to school. You have to walk six blocks in 90° heat to the school bus stop. Sorry, but that's nothing.

Rick Hansen of Canada wheeled his wheelchair 24,901.55 miles. He crossed 34 countries and four continents. It took him over two years. George Meegan of Great Britain walked from the southern tip of South America to Prudhoe Bay in Alaska. That's 19,019 miles and 2,426 days. Plennie Wingo walked backwards from Santa Monica, California, to Istanbul, Turkey—over 8,000 miles. Each of these people faced a huge *challenge*. With the help of many people, each one met the challenge.

---

1. The best title is—
   (A) The Long Way Home
   (B) Lost in the Country
   (C) Driving Across America
   (D) A Nice Day

2. Rick Hansen wheeled his wheelchair through—
   (A) 7 countries (B) 2 continents
   (C) 34 countries (D) 3 continents

3. Plennie Wingo walked backwards for about—
   (A) 34,000 miles (B) 8,000 miles
   (C) 19,000 miles (D) 4 miles

4. You can tell that these people were—
   (A) lazy (B) happy
   (C) determined (D) sad

5. The word "challenge" in line eleven means—
   (A) offer (B) test
   (C) walk (D) accident

UNIT 11

Karen bounced the basketball to Ellen. In a flash, Ellen had tossed the ball through the hoop. The Tigers were back in the lead again!

Karen and Ellen had been playing ball together for almost two years. At first, it had been hard for them to learn how to move their wheelchairs around the court. Now, though, they were the Tigers' very best players. They had even helped their team become the state wheelchair basketball champions. Tonight they planned to become the champions again.

"Let's go!" cried Karen as she grabbed the ball and wheeled toward the basket. Her team was on its way to another *victory*.

---

1. The best title is—
   (A) Girls' Basketball
   (B) Ellen's Story
   (C) The Wheelchair Basketball Winners
   (D) Boys Playing in Wheelchairs

2. Karen and Ellen play wheelchair basketball—
   (A) for the Tigers
   (B) for the Lions
   (C) only with each other
   (D) on different teams

3. At first, the girls thought the game was—
   (A) easy
   (B) silly
   (C) not easy
   (D) scary

4. Karen and Ellen cannot—
   (A) win
   (B) throw
   (C) move
   (D) walk

5. The word "victory" in line ten means—
   (A) basket
   (B) win
   (C) race
   (D) game

UNIT 12

Mr. Coates worked in a music store. In the store there were many old instruments that no one *cared* to buy. Most of them were made of brass. Mr. Coates bought the old musical instruments and took them home. He didn't use them to play music—he made lamps out of them!

First, Mr. Coates cleaned and polished the instruments. Then he put light bulbs on them, and a wire to plug them in. Finally, he put a lampshade over each bulb. All the lamps worked.

Mr. Coates says, "I have the most unusual lamps in the world."

---

1. The best title is—
   (A) Playing in the School Band
   (B) A Wonderful Band
   (C) Listening to Good Music
   (D) Lamps Made of Musical Instruments

2. Most of the musical instruments were made of—
   (A) wool (B) brass
   (C) iron (D) glass

3. All the lamps that Mr. Coates made—
   (A) were stolen (B) fell apart
   (C) caught fire (D) worked

4. When Mr. Coates first bought the instruments, they were—
   (A) flat (B) clean
   (C) dirty (D) used as tables

5. The word "cared" in line two means—
   (A) smelled (B) wanted
   (C) whistled (D) climbed

In Unit 10, you read about several long trips. There are many other kinds of trips. You can visit parks and museums. You can travel to cities you have never seen before.

A trip can be a lot of fun. You can travel by car or plane or even by boat. You can travel just a few miles or many miles. You can stay for just a day or for many days. On a trip you can learn many new facts about the places you visit.

A. Exercising Your Skill

Think about a trip you might like to take. It can be to any place in the world. Where would you go? Think about all of these things. Now look at the idea map below. Make a larger copy of it on a sheet of paper. What is the question in each center circle? Read the questions. Then think of two or three facts to answer each question. Write a different answer in each empty circle around the question.

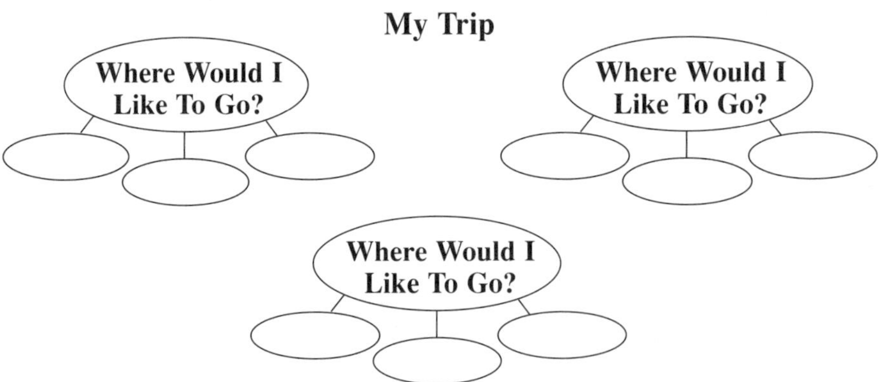

B. Expanding Your Skill

Here are some more questions to answer when you are planning a trip: How will I travel? When will I go? Where will I stay? How long will I stay?

Add two of these questions to your idea map. Write three answers to each question. (If you need more room, write the new questions on another sheet of paper.)

C. Exploring Language

Imagine that you are taking a trip to Holiday Land. Holiday Land has a zoo, a lake for swimming and boating, and woods where you can hike. Use your own words to complete this postcard. In some blanks you may use more than one word. Write the postcard on your paper.

> *Dear _____ ,*
>
> *Holiday Land is _____ ! All morning we _____ . Then we went to _____ . Guess what we saw there! A _____ ! It was _____ . Later we cooked our own dinner. We made _____ . So far, the best part of this vacation has been _____ . When I come home, I will show you _____ .*
>
> *Your friend,*
>
> _____

D. Expressing Yourself

Choose one of these things.

1. Write a few facts about a place you visited. Answer these questions. Use complete sentences.
   - Where did I go?
   - How did I get there?
   - What did I do and see?
   - What did I like? What didn't I like?
2. Make a postcard of a place to visit. It can be a real place or one you make up. On half a sheet of white paper, draw a colorful picture of the place. Then turn the paper over and write a greeting to a friend. Tell your friend about the place.

UNIT 13

Mrs. Hoskins had a dream. In her dream she sold her house and bought a motor home. A motor home is something like a small truck—with beds, a kitchen, and often even a TV set. When Mrs. Hoskins woke up, she went out and sold her house and bought a motor home. Then she and her fifteen-year-old son went on a trip.

They traveled 28,000 miles. They went across the United States, through Mexico and Canada, and to Alaska. Mrs. Hoskins and her son said it was a *glorious* trip. They were glad that she had her dream.

---

1. The best title is—
   (A) A Trip by Motor Home
   (B) Watching TV
   (C) The Indians of Mexico
   (D) A Long Bicycle Ride

2. The story says that a motor home has—
   (A) no windows
   (B) a library
   (C) beds
   (D) sails

3. Mrs. Hoskins and her son traveled through—
   (A) Africa
   (B) Italy
   (C) England
   (D) Canada

4. Mrs. Hoskins bought a motor home because—
   (A) her house burned down
   (B) she had a dream
   (C) it was winter
   (D) her son was sick

5. The word "glorious" in line eight means—
   (A) sleeping
   (B) ugly
   (C) terrible
   (D) wonderful

UNIT 14

Mr. Weiss had a pet cat. Its name was Kat. Kat had a wonderful life. It was fed only the best food—fish, chicken, liver, and warm milk. Kat was the happiest pet in town. Then Mr. Weiss died. He left Kat over $6,000 so that the animal could always live a *comfortable* life.

Kat went to live with one of Mr. Weiss' friends. The friend thought that the cat was eating too much, and eating the wrong kinds of food. She fed Kat only cat food and cold milk. From then on, Kat ate the same foods that most cats eat—even though the pet had more than $6,000 in the bank!

---

1. The best title is—
   (A) How Kat's Life Changed
   (B) Making Cat Food
   (C) A Home for Pets
   (D) Cats Are Smart Animals

2. Kat used to eat—
   (A) hot dogs (B) peanuts
   (C) fish (D) popcorn

3. Mr. Weiss' friend thought that Kat—
   (A) should be in a zoo (B) could sing
   (C) was a dog (D) was eating too much

4. You can tell that Mr. Weiss—
   (A) was very poor (B) hated animals
   (C) loved his pet (D) had no friends

5. The word "comfortable" in line five means—
   (A) dangerous (B) easy
   (C) hard (D) short

UNIT 15

People all over the world know how Paul Bunyan cut down trees to clear the forests of the American Midwest. Stories of this giant are found in books, songs, and even cartoons. It is easy to picture people sitting in old logging camps telling "tall tales" about Paul and his pet blue ox, Babe.

Paul Bunyan did not come from tall tales, though. He was made up by a man named W.B. Laughead, who wrote ads for newspapers and magazines. Laughead *invented* the giant and his pet ox in the 1920s as part of an ad for the Red River Lumber Company. Can you think of any made-up (or real!) person in today's ads who might become a great American hero?

---

1. The best title is—
   - (A) Paul Bunyan Clears the Great Plains
   - (B) Tall Tales
   - (C) How Paul Bunyan Came to Be
   - (D) Babe, the Blue Ox

2. Paul Bunyan was a giant who—
   - (A) wrote ads
   - (B) planted forests
   - (C) cut down trees
   - (D) raised cows

3. W.B. Laughead made up Paul Bunyan for a—
   - (A) cartoon
   - (B) lumber ad
   - (C) tall tale
   - (D) book about America

4. Laughead did not know that Paul Bunyan would—
   - (A) be in an ad
   - (B) have a pet ox
   - (C) be a giant
   - (D) become a hero

5. The word "invented" in line eight means—
   - (A) sold
   - (B) wanted
   - (C) made up
   - (D) saw

UNIT 16

Harry Bradley was getting on an airplane. He turned and saw a group of children looking at the plane. He heard one of them say, "I hope that I can ride in an airplane someday." Harry began to think of all the children who had never ridden in a plane.

When he got home, Harry called an airport. He said, "I want to rent a big airplane." Then he took a group of schoolchildren for a long ride.

Harry gave airplane rides to hundreds of girls and boys. The children rode free because Harry paid all the *expenses*.

---

1. The best title is—
   (A) Flying Around the World
   (B) Airplane Rides for Children
   (C) Making Airplanes Safe
   (D) A Busy Airport

2. Harry gave airplane rides to hundreds of—
   (A) women (B) children
   (C) pets (D) men

3. For the children, the plane rides were—
   (A) dangerous (B) no fun
   (C) free (D) short

4. You can tell that Harry Bradley—
   (A) hated airplanes (B) was poor
   (C) could not see (D) liked children

5. The word "expenses" in line nine means—
   (A) costs (B) books
   (C) ice cream (D) accidents

UNIT 17

In 1977, Sophia Collier set out to make a new kind of soft drink. Like many other people, she was upset that soft drinks often had in them things that were not healthful. Still, she enjoyed the taste of a soda now and then. That was why she decided to make a soft drink that was healthful.

Collier tried long and hard. She *labored* for hours in the kitchen of her Brooklyn, New York, apartment. Finally, she found a way to make soda that was healthful but still tasted good. Today, Collier's company makes millions of dollars each year selling healthful soft drinks.

---

1. The best title is—
   (A) The Bad Taste of Sodas
   (B) An Unusual Soft Drink
   (C) Hard Work Doesn't Pay
   (D) Natural Foods

2. Collier began work in—
   (A) the spring (B) a school
   (C) 1977 (D) a factory

3. Collier decided to make soft drinks that were—
   (A) healthful (B) fruit-flavored
   (C) cheap (D) canned

4. You can tell that many people—
   (A) do not like soda (B) like Sophia Collier
   (C) drink fruit juice (D) like Collier's soda

5. The word "labored" in line six means—
   (A) waited (B) worked
   (C) washed (D) hurried

UNIT 18

Cats sometimes climb so high in trees that they are afraid to climb down. If someone doesn't help them, they may fall and get badly hurt. Years ago, fire fighters used their ladders to save the helpless cats. Today, the fire fighters are usually too busy to help.

The cats on Long Island are lucky. Paul Petzold's job is climbing trees to *snip* off dead branches. Paul, however, likes cats. He will always take the time to climb a tree to save a frightened cat. He has even rescued cats at night and during the winter. Paul is a person who really loves cats.

---

1. The best title is—
   (A) How to Climb a Ladder
   (B) A Man Who Saves Cats
   (C) Finding a Lost Dog
   (D) People Who Put Out Fires

2. The story says that Paul has rescued cats—
   (A) in an airplane (B) at night
   (C) from burning houses (D) in Canada

3. The story says that cats are afraid if they—
   (A) eat too fast (B) meet a mouse
   (C) hear a bird (D) climb too high

4. You can tell that Paul—
   (A) has a pet dog (B) is a good climber
   (C) has two cars (D) hates animals

5. The word "snip" in line six means—
   (A) grow (B) look
   (C) cut (D) feel

UNIT 19

Most newspapers are too *difficult* for children to read. Betty Debnam decided that there should be a page just for children in the newspaper. She wrote a page about things that children like and put it in her town's newspaper. She called it the "Mini Page." The children in her town loved it. So did their parents.

Soon other newspapers wanted to use the Mini Page. Betty began writing the special page for children every week. Over the years more than two hundred different newspapers have had a Mini Page.

Have you ever seen the Mini Page? If not, maybe you can find a way to start one.

---

1. The best title is—
   (A) Learning to Read
   (B) How to Write a Story
   (C) A Newspaper Page for Children
   (D) A School That Sells Newspapers

2. Over the years, the Mini Page has been in more than—
   (A) 500 newspapers (B) 50 magazines
   (C) 100 books (D) 200 newspapers

3. The Mini Page was written for—
   (A) teachers (B) parents
   (C) children (D) babies

4. The Mini Page probably had—
   (A) easy words (B) no pictures
   (C) terrible stories (D) green print

5. The word "difficult" in line one means—
   (A) easy (B) hard
   (C) funny (D) short

UNIT 20

How would you like to be in the water and have sharks only a few inches away? Most people would not, but in Australia, people even pay to be that close to sharks!

Rodney Fox is one person who has taken many people to meet sharks. First, Rodney takes you out on the ocean in his boat. Then he throws horsemeat into the water to bring the sharks near the boat. Next, you are put into a steel cage and lowered into the ocean. People who have taken the trip say that the sharks *bang* against the cage and even stick their noses inside!

---

1. The best title is—
   (A) Eating Horsemeat
   (B) Fishing in Australia
   (C) Meeting Sharks
   (D) The Boats of Australia

2. To ride with Rodney, you have to go to—
   (A) India (B) Canada
   (C) Norway (D) Australia

3. When you meet the sharks, you are in a—
   (A) wooden box (B) steel cage
   (C) small boat (D) large room

4. The story suggests that sharks like to eat—
   (A) boats (B) plants
   (C) horsemeat (D) steel cages

5. The word "bang" in line eight means—
   (A) fish (B) eat
   (C) bump (D) look

UNIT 21

Parents often have trouble deciding what to name a new baby. They usually want a name that sounds nice. Sometimes they name their baby after an aunt or grandfather. Mr. and Mrs. Flower wanted to give their baby a name that was *original*—a name that no one else ever had!

When their baby was born, Mr. and Mrs. Flower thought for many hours before they decided on a name for their baby daughter. She had been born on a Sunday, the third of May. So they named their little girl "Sunday May Third Flower."

Their daughter is happy that her friends just call her "Sunny."

---

1. The best title is—
   (A) Mrs. Flower Goes Away
   (B) A Girl with an Unusual Name
   (C) Mr. Flower's Grandfather
   (D) A Tiny Baby

2. The Flowers' daughter was born in—
   (A) July
   (B) June
   (C) April
   (D) May

3. The girl's friends call her—
   (A) Third
   (B) Friday
   (C) Sunny
   (D) Rose

4. The girl's real name tells—
   (A) where she lives
   (B) what she looks like
   (C) when she was born
   (D) where she was born

5. The word "original" in line four means—
   (A) new
   (B) afraid
   (C) short
   (D) quiet

UNIT 22

Whales are probably the largest and strongest animals in the world. Perhaps that is why it is hard to think that a whale might need *assistance* from people.

Yet, in recent years, people have had to rescue several whales from some real trouble. One whale, for example, found itself in the Hudson River. Without help from the people of New York, the whale might have remained there forever. Another whale got stuck in the harbor at San Francisco, California. For several days, the world watched as people and boats helped the whale make its way back to the open sea.

---

1. The best title is—
   (A) How Whales Help People
   (B) People Helping Whales
   (C) The Hudson River Whale
   (D) California, Here I Come

2. One whale was stuck in—
   (A) the mud
   (B) a trap
   (C) Arctic ice
   (D) San Francisco harbor

3. People helped a whale—
   (A) learn to breathe
   (B) get back to sea
   (C) find a home
   (D) have babies

4. You can tell that the Hudson River is in—
   (A) California
   (B) San Francisco
   (C) New York
   (D) Europe

5. The word "assistance" in line three means—
   (A) happiness
   (B) food
   (C) help
   (D) trouble

UNIT 23

One day, Mrs. Rhoads saw a little dog. She petted the dog and then went home. The dog followed her. Mrs. Rhoads didn't want a pet, so she left it outside. The next morning the dog was still there—*wagging* its tail back and forth.

Mrs. Rhoads took the dog across town and gave it to a friend. The next day it was back. She gave the dog away three times, but it always returned.

Mrs. Rhoads couldn't give the dog away, so she decided to keep it. Besides, she was getting to love the little dog that always returned.

---

1. The best title is—
   (A) Looking for a Lost Dog
   (B) A Trip Across Town
   (C) A Dog That Always Returned
   (D) A Woman Trains Her Pet

2. When Mrs. Rhoads first saw the dog, she—
   (A) chased it (B) bought it
   (C) fed it (D) petted it

3. Mrs. Rhoads once gave the dog to a—
   (A) police officer (B) friend
   (C) school (D) farmer

4. The little dog must have—
   (A) been sick (B) been old
   (C) liked Mrs. Rhoads (D) hated Mrs. Rhoads

5. The word "wagging" in line four means—
   (A) moving (B) biting
   (C) cleaning (D) finding

UNIT 24

A truck was speeding down a highway as it came to a curve in the road. It was going too fast to make the turn. The truck hit the side of the road and *overturned*. Out came everything it was carrying—sixty thousand hamburgers!

Students from a nearby school ran over to the truck. The driver said, "If you will pick up all these small boxes of hamburgers, I'll give your school a present." The students spent five hours picking up the hamburgers. The hamburgers were saved, and the driver gave the school $300. The money was used to buy equipment for the playground.

---

1. The best title is—
   (A) A Ride in a Bus
   (B) Students Pick Up Hamburgers
   (C) Building a New School
   (D) Eating Hamburgers for Lunch

2. The hamburgers were in—
   (A) paper bags (B) cloth bags
   (C) red socks (D) small boxes

3. The story says that the hamburgers were—
   (A) eaten by dogs (B) run over by cars
   (C) saved (D) lost

4. The truck in the story must have been—
   (A) made of glass (B) large
   (C) blue (D) going slowly

5. The word "overturned" in line three means—
   (A) won the race (B) cooked
   (C) tipped over (D) caught fire

The Second L A P
Language Activity Pages

In Unit 23, you read about how one woman found just the right pet for herself. Read below about another kind of pet. As you read, pay special attention to the underlined words.

> Would you like a talking pet? If you would, you should consider the idea of buying a parrot. A dog can only bark, a cat can only meow, but a parrot can utter words. Parrots do not really comprehend the meanings of words. Yet they speak quite distinctly, so you can tell just what they are saying. Teaching a parrot to speak is not a very demanding job. In fact, it is very easy. You just say the same words again and again. Soon the parrot will mimic you.

A. Exercising Your Skill

In the sentences above, some words are underlined. Do you know the meanings of those words? If you do not, you might be able to figure out the meanings. Look for clues in the rest of the sentence and in the other sentences. Now see if you can find the meanings in the box below.

clearly	say	copy	think about	understand	hard

Copy the list below on a piece of paper. Beside each word, write the correct meaning from the box above.

Word	Meaning	Word	Meaning
1. consider	______	4. distinctly	______
2. utter	______	5. demanding	______
3. comprehend	______	6. mimic	______

B. Expanding Your Skill

How many words do you know that name different kinds of animals? At the top of your paper, write the three labels. Under each label, write all the animal names that you can think of.

Pets   Farm Animals   Wild Animals

C. Exploring Language

Each sentence below has a missing word. The other words in the sentence will give you clues. Number your paper from 1 through 10. Then write the words you think best fill the blanks.

Some people are scared of all snakes, but many snakes are not (1)_____. In fact, some snakes are even kept as (2) _____. Their owners hold them or (3) _____ the snakes around their necks and shoulders. You may think that a snake's skin feels (4)_____, but really it is quite dry. Snake owners keep their snakes in glass tanks, along with moss, grass, and other (5)_____. If you buy a snake at a pet (6)_____, be sure to find out how to care for your new pet. You will need to know the (7)_____ to these questions: What kinds of (8)_____ does this snake eat? Does it need to (9)_____water? Would my snake rather be in a warm place or a (10) _____place?

D. Expressing Yourself

Choose one of these things.

1. What kind of pet would you like? Begin by drawing a picture of a pet you would like to have. Under the picture, write three or four sentences about why you think this animal would make a wonderful pet.

2. In the library, find a book about different kinds of animals. Which animal seems the most unusual or interesting to you? Read about this animal, and try to find answers to all of the questions below. Write each question with its answer on your paper.

   - What is the animal's name?
   - What does it look like?
   - What does it eat?
   - How large is it?
   - Where does it live?
   - What other facts interest you?

UNIT 25

Kids love to visit Dr. Greenberg, even though he is a dentist. This is because he likes to have fun, and he wants the children to have fun too.

While they are waiting for their turn to see the dentist, the children can listen to rock'n'roll music or even play their own records. When their turn comes, they are usually surprised, because Dr. Greenberg likes to dress in costumes. Sometimes he dresses like Superman, a clown, or Mickey Mouse. Sometimes he even dresses in very old clothes.

Besides making the visits *entertaining*, Dr. Greenberg is a good dentist.

---

1. The best title is—
   (A) Costumes Can Be Fun
   (B) How to Care for Your Teeth
   (C) A Dentist Who's Fun to Visit
   (D) The Best Kind of Music

2. Dr. Greenberg sometimes dresses like—
   (A) Donald Duck
   (B) Superman
   (C) a monkey
   (D) a police officer

3. The story says that Dr. Greenberg likes to—
   (A) go fishing
   (B) watch TV
   (C) play the piano
   (D) have fun

4. Dr. Greenberg is probably a—
   (A) mean person
   (B) movie star
   (C) schoolteacher
   (D) nice man

5. The word "entertaining" in line ten means—
   (A) impossible
   (B) fun
   (C) cheap
   (D) terrible

UNIT 26

It is not very unusual for a sports person to win more than one medal in the Olympic Games. Swimmers Mark Spitz and Matt Biondi, for example, have each won five or more medals.

It is unusual, however, for two people in the same family to each win more than one Olympic medal in one year. This was *accomplished* in 1988 by two American women, Florence Griffith-Joyner and Jackie Joyner-Kersee. The two women are sisters-in-law—and Olympic champions. Griffith-Joyner became famous when she won both the 100-meter and 200-meter races. Her sister-in-law amazed the world with her wins in the long jump and the difficult heptathlon.

---

1. The best title is—
   (A) The Heptathlon
   (B) Two Champions in the Family
   (C) Florence Griffith-Joyner
   (D) Olympic Swimming Records

2. Mark Spitz won—
   (A) two skating contests
   (B) foot races
   (C) the long jump
   (D) swimming races

3. Jackie Joyner-Kersee won in the—
   (A) 100-meter race
   (B) 200-meter race
   (C) high dive
   (D) long jump

4. You can tell that both women are—
   (A) very good in sports
   (B) short
   (C) well liked
   (D) the same age

5. The word "accomplished" in line six means—
   (A) lost
   (B) remembered
   (C) done
   (D) begun

UNIT 27

Animals can become famous for many different reasons. One cow, for example, is known because of one of the worst *disasters* in history. The event, often called "the Great Chicago Fire," began in a barn that belonged to a woman named Mrs. O'Leary. Within minutes, buildings all over the city were on fire. Much of the city was burned.

Afterwards, officials and newspaper writers tried to find out just how the fire in Mrs. O'Leary's barn had gotten started. Most of them agreed that Mrs. O'Leary's cow must have knocked over a gas lamp. The straw and hay in the building had quickly caught fire.

---

1. The best title is—
   (A) A Cow, a Lamp, and a Fire
   (B) The History of Chicago
   (C) The Fire That Stopped
   (D) Mrs. O'Leary

2. The fire began in a—
   (A) field (B) department store
   (C) barn (D) gas station

3. The cow knocked over a—
   (A) heater (B) lamp
   (C) candle (D) stool

4. You can tell that the cause of the fire was—
   (A) a person (B) an accident
   (C) a cold wind (D) lightning

5. The word "disasters" in line two means—
   (A) arguments (B) cities
   (C) holidays (D) terrible events

UNIT 28

Since 1874, four buildings have had the name Madison Square Garden.

The first building, on Madison Avenue between 26th and 27th Streets, was called the Great Roman Hippodrome. It was built by P. T. Barnum to *house* his circus. When he sold it in 1879, the name was changed to Madison Square Garden. The first building was torn down in 1889, and a new building opened in 1890. At one time, this second building was turned into a swimming pool that held 1,500,000 gallons of water.

The third Madison Square Garden opened in 1925. It was located on Eighth Avenue between 49th and 50th Streets. It went up in only 249 days. The fourth Madison Square Garden opened in 1968. The New York Knicks won their first NBA title on May 8, 1970, at this Madison Square Garden.

---

1. The best title is—
   (A) Play Ball
   (B) The Greatest Circus
   (C) The New York Knicks
   (D) Four Madison Square Gardens

2. The second Madison Square Garden—
   (A) was torn down in 1889
   (B) once had a swimming pool
   (C) is 100 years old
   (D) had a climbing wall

3. The latest Madison Square Garden opened in—
   (A) 1970
   (B) 1929
   (C) 1968
   (D) 1890

4. You can tell that the name Madison Square Garden—
   (A) was destroyed
   (B) means "boxing"
   (C) won't last
   (D) is important to people

5. The word "house" in line five means—
   (A) cover
   (B) hold
   (C) carry
   (D) tent

UNIT 29

When the spacecraft Apollo 16 landed on the moon in December 1972, George Carruthers was not part of the crew. Carruthers, though, was very important to the event in a different way.

Born in 1940, Carruthers is one of this country's leading scientists. For many years, he worked on America's space program. He made a special tool that could be used to find out exactly what the rocks and the dust on the moon were made of. In 1972, this special tool *accompanied* the Apollo 16 crew to the moon. The tool that Carruthers made helped scientists understand the moon better than ever before.

---

1. The best title is—
   (A) Apollo 16
   (B) George Carruthers, Space Scientist
   (C) Travels in Outer Space
   (D) Learning About Rocks

2. Carruthers is—
   (A) a moon walker
   (B) an army officer
   (C) a carpenter
   (D) a scientist

3. Apollo 16—
   (A) was built in 1940
   (B) went to Mars
   (C) landed on the moon
   (D) is a TV show

4. You can tell that the flight of Apollo 16—
   (A) changed the moon
   (B) took many weeks
   (C) returned to Earth
   (D) had many problems

5. The word "accompanied" in line eight means—
   (A) visited
   (B) went with
   (C) listened to
   (D) waited for

UNIT 30

"Sometimes I can't believe how exciting my job is," says Denise Gould. "Building things is a real thrill."

Gould's *occupation* is building houses. What makes it so exciting? No two houses that she builds are alike. Before Gould starts building, she spends hours talking with her customers. When she understands exactly what they want, she begins building their perfect "dream house."

Some of her houses look as if they come from the future. Others look as if they have been around for hundreds of years. Her favorite, though, was built for a family that loved boats. It is shaped just like a sailboat. "It makes us feel we're always on our boat," says the owner.

---

1. The best title is—
   (A) Houses like Boats
   (B) New Houses for You
   (C) Denise Gould: Dream-house Builder
   (D) Jobs in Home Building for Boat Lovers

2. Some of Denise Gould's houses look—
   (A) very old
   (B) like spaceships
   (C) alike
   (D) like bad dreams

3. One of her houses—
   (A) is on the ocean
   (B) is falling apart
   (C) looks like a boat
   (D) looks like a castle

4. You can tell that Denise Gould likes to—
   (A) earn a lot of money
   (B) please her customers
   (C) build boats
   (D) make friends

5. The word "occupation" in line three means—
   (A) time
   (B) game
   (C) plan
   (D) job

UNIT 31

Twelve-year-old Danny Leardi had an unusual weekend job. Every Saturday morning, he drove with his father to the dock at Sheepshead Bay in Brooklyn, New York. There Danny helped with his father's boat, *Skipjack III*.

Skipjack III was a fishing boat. Each day that the weather was good, it took people fishing on the Atlantic Ocean. On weekends and days when there was no school, Danny went along. He did everything from selling tickets to *baiting* hooks to cleaning fish. "It's great," Danny said. "I get to meet all kinds of people. And if I miss being able to do things with my friends, I just invite them to come along."

---

1. The best title is—
   (A) Danny and His Dad
   (B) The One That Got Away
   (C) An Unusual Weekend Job
   (D) Fishing

2. Danny—
   (A) sold fish (B) sold tickets
   (C) worked on school days (D) owned a boat

3. On the boat, Danny—
   (A) sat on the edge (B) cooked fish dinners
   (C) took naps (D) cleaned fish

4. You can tell that the passengers—
   (A) usually got seasick (B) didn't like fishing
   (C) paid for their trip (D) did not like Danny

5. The word "baiting" in line eight means—
   (A) putting food on (B) carrying
   (C) watching (D) cleaning

UNIT 32

Jennie Ruiz is a computer whiz. When she was only four years old, she began using her brother's computer. Just using the computer was not enough for Jennie, though. Soon, she was making up her own computer games. She would get an idea for a game. Then she would write a program for it. News about Jennie's exciting games spread quickly.

Now, Jennie has her own computer business. She *creates* games, puts them in colorful boxes, and sells them in stores all over the area. "That's just the beginning," she says, pointing to a keyboard and screen on her desk. "Soon I'll be selling the Jennie 1," she says. "It's fantastic. And it's just for kids."

---

1. The best title is—
   (A) How to Write Your Own Computer Games
   (B) Computer Games
   (C) Jennie Ruiz, Computer Whiz
   (D) Young People in Business

2. The first computer Jennie used—
   (A) broke quickly
   (B) came from school
   (C) was her brother's
   (D) was a birthday gift

3. Jennie sells her games—
   (A) to her family
   (B) by mail
   (C) by telephone
   (D) in stores

4. You can tell that the Jennie 1 is a—
   (A) computer
   (B) television
   (C) typewriter
   (D) business

5. The word "creates" in line seven means—
   (A) sells
   (B) plays
   (C) makes
   (D) learns

UNIT 33

Today's telephones can do more than just put you in touch with another person. They can also provide you with a number of handy services.

When the phone rings, do you ever ask yourself, "Who is it? Is it for me?" Some telephones show you the telephone number of the phone from which the call is being placed. That way, if you *recognize* the number, you know who is calling.

When a line is busy, do you waste a lot of time calling again and again? Some telephones will keep calling the number all by themselves until someone finally answers the phone.

---

1. The best title is—
   (A) Liking Other People
   (B) Today's Handy Telephones
   (C) Telephones, Old and New
   (D) Why Telephones Break

2. One phone service shows you the caller's—
   (A) face (B) address
   (C) name (D) telephone number

3. One phone service keeps calling again when—
   (A) the line is busy (B) no one is home
   (C) you forget to call (D) the phone is broken

4. The "calling again" service is—
   (A) for business only (B) not yet in use
   (C) for saving you time (D) for night use only

5. The word "recognize" in line seven means—
   (A) write (B) sing
   (C) like (D) know

UNIT 34

Many people came to Marcella's party. She was sixty years old and was quitting her job to rest. There were a *bouquet* of flowers and a large cake at the party. The cake was in the shape of an elephant—because Marcella was an elephant!

Marcella had worked in the circus for fifty-five years. She had been in 29,700 shows. The seven-thousand-pound elephant enjoyed her party. She ate the whole cake all by herself. Then she ate the flowers!

Marcella was sent to a park for animals. There she could rest and eat all she wanted.

---

1. The best title is—
   (A) A Boy Joins the Circus
   (B) How to Ride an Elephant
   (C) An Elephant Runs Away
   (D) An Elephant Has a Party

2. Marcella had worked in the circus for—
   (A) 2 years (B) 55 years
   (C) 100 years (D) 40 years

3. At the party, Marcella ate—
   (A) an apple (B) a chair
   (C) hay (D) a cake

4. At her new home in the park, Marcella had—
   (A) a swimming pool (B) an easy life
   (C) nothing to eat (D) no time to sleep

5. The word "bouquet" in line two means—
   (A) bunch (B) pen
   (C) zoo (D) smell

UNIT 35

During the winter, Fred Carpenter goes skiing just about every weekend. Sometimes he drives as far as three hundred miles to find the freshest snow. Then he unpacks his gear and heads for the slopes.

Fred has been skiing since he was seven years old. By the time he was twelve, he had won several junior championships. When he was thirteen, he lost his right leg in an accident. By the next season, Fred had learned to ski on one leg. "It's certainly a little harder this way," Fred says, "but the thrill is just the same."

Now Fred is looking for other people like himself who love to ski. "It's time to *organize* some races!" he says.

---

1. The best title is—
   (A) Racing on Skis
   (B) Learning to Ski
   (C) Three Hundred Miles of Snow
   (D) Fred Carpenter: Ski Champion

2. Fred Carpenter began skiing when he was—
   (A) twelve (B) thirteen
   (C) fourteen (D) seven

3. Carpenter learned to ski—
   (A) in the hospital (B) on an icy lake
   (C) on one leg (D) in Canada

4. Fred Carpenter does not—
   (A) love skiing (B) give up easily
   (C) enjoy racing (D) like excitement

5. The word "organize" in line ten means—
   (A) remember (B) plan
   (C) stop (D) leave

UNIT 36

"Did you know," Randy's teacher asked, "that many of the things we throw away can be used again? Using old papers, cans, and bottles to make new things is called recycling."

The class decided to set up their own recycling center. They collected big crates, painted them, and set them out near the school. Red crates were for bottles and blue ones were for cans. Others were for newspapers.

Students and their families *deposited* garbage in the crates. When the crates were full, trucks came and took the garbage to factories. There, it was used to make new bottles, cans, and newspapers. The factories even paid the class for the garbage.

---

1. The best title is—
   (A) Randy's Class
   (B) Things to Make with Paper
   (C) A Useful Class Project
   (D) Recycling Bottles

2. Bottles were put in—
   (A) old newspapers (B) blue crates
   (C) buses (D) red crates

3. Trucks collected—
   (A) presents (B) garbage
   (C) milk (D) oil

4. Recycling keeps things from being—
   (A) broken (B) wasted
   (C) forgotten (D) used

5. The word "deposited" in line eight means—
   (A) took (B) dug
   (C) put (D) closed

UNIT 37

The audience clapped and cheered as Ted Hon put down his instrument, a saxophone. "We'll take a break now," Ted announced, "but our band will be back *shortly*."

Ted's band plays an unusual kind of music. "Our music sounds different from the music other groups play," Ted explains. "I'm from Hawaii. My mother is Hawaiian, and my father is Japanese. Chris, our drum player, is from a Chinese family. Our piano player's family settled in California in 1850. We're all really interested in the music of China and Japan. I guess that's why the music we play has a special sound." If the audience at this concert is any sign, there will soon be a lot more interest in Ted Hon's band and its music.

---

1. The best title is—
   (A) Playing in a Band
   (B) The Story of Hawaii
   (C) Ted Hon's Band
   (D) Music of the East

2. Ted Hon is from—
   (A) Hawaii
   (B) Japan
   (C) New York
   (D) California

3. The band is interested in the music of—
   (A) the East Coast
   (B) California
   (C) China and Japan
   (D) Hawaii

4. Ted probably first learned about Japan—
   (A) by playing music
   (B) from his father
   (C) during a trip
   (D) in school

5. The word "shortly" in line three means—
   (A) often
   (B) soon
   (C) nearly
   (D) one at a time

UNIT 38

"Come on, let's get going!" Maryanne's father called. "We'll be late for the party."

"I'm coming," Maryanne cried. She was trying to get Sparks back into the house. Sparks never liked to be left behind when the family went away. Today he was behaving worse than usual.

Finally, Maryanne dashed to the car. She tossed her aunt's birthday present into the trunk and slipped into the back seat. "Go!" she cried.

Fifteen minutes later, the sound of barking came from the trunk. Maryanne's father gave Maryanne a *dismayed* look. He stopped the car. They got out and opened the trunk. "Sparks must have jumped into the trunk," Maryanne said. "He hates to be left alone."

---

1. The best title is—
   (A) The Birthday Party
   (B) Maryanne
   (C) An Unwanted Passenger
   (D) Taking Care of Your Puppy

2. The family was going to—
   (A) the park
   (B) a party
   (C) dinner
   (D) a movie

3. Sparks did not like—
   (A) being outdoors
   (B) Maryanne's father
   (C) riding in cars
   (D) being left behind

4. You can tell that Sparks is—
   (A) a cat
   (B) Maryanne's brother
   (C) a dog
   (D) a parakeet

5. The word "dismayed" in line nine means—
   (A) careless
   (B) unhappy
   (C) pleased
   (D) thankful

In Unit 33, you read about some wonderful new inventions. Here is information about some other inventions.

Have you ever had an idea for an invention? Perhaps you thought of a machine that could do a certain job. Perhaps you had an idea for something fun to play with. Not long ago, children living near Boston had a chance to show off their best inventions. For example, Erich Streisand showed his "automatic page turner." Erich's machine uses a magnet to turn the pages of a book. Lindsey Cotter's "dry-feet bird feeder" lets birds get at their food without having to stand in puddles or snow. Michael Grenier's "tippy chair" moves without falling over. After the "Inventors Weekend," four of the young people were guests on a late-night TV talk show.

A. Exercising Your Skill

Many people make new inventions. Think about the examples of inventions made by children for the "Inventors Weekend." Read the two lists below. On your paper, write a name (heading) telling the main idea of each list.

INVENTORS WEEKEND

(Heading)	*(Heading)*
scientists	automatic page turner
children	dry-feet bird feeder
people with imagination	tippy chair

B. Expanding Your Skill

What new things do you think should be invented? What would they be like? Write the names of two new "inventions" on your paper. Below each name, write a sentence telling what that invention could do.

C. Exploring Language

Each paragraph below has a main idea and details that tell about it. Read each paragraph. On your paper, write a title that tells readers the main idea of the paragraph.

(Title)

1. One of the most interesting things at "Inventors Weekend" was a special desk. This desk was built by Larry Simonetti and Dusten Peterson. Just about everything you would ever want has been built into this desk—even lights. In fact, the only thing it can't do for you is your homework!

(Title)

2. Young Kimberly Sims showed her new invention—a "two-door mailbox." A letter carrier puts mail in the front door. Then all you have to do is open the back door of the mailbox to pull out your mail.

D. Expressing Yourself

Choose one of these activities.

1. Write a newspaper article that tells about an "Inventors Weekend" held in your town. In your story, tell things such as what the fair was about, what kinds of inventions were shown, and how people felt about what they saw.
2. Describe an invention you would like to make. Use one of the ideas you wrote in Part B or think of a new idea. Give the invention a name. Write a main idea sentence and three or four sentences that give details about the main idea. Tell what your invention does, whom it will help, and how you could go about making the invention.

UNIT 39

Elephants are the largest animals that live on land. The elephants that lived on earth thousands of years ago are called mammoths.

About twelve years ago, a worker was digging near an apartment building. He found some large bones. Scientists came to look at the bones. They said that they were the bones of a mammoth that lived fourteen thousand years ago! Everyone was excited. Hundreds of people watched as workers dug up the bones. Even schoolchildren came on buses to watch.

The bones of this mammoth that lived *ages* ago are now in a museum.

---

1. The best title is—
   (A) What Elephants Look Like
   (B) Finding the Bones of a Mammoth
   (C) Why Schoolchildren Ride Buses
   (D) Caring for Elephants

2. Elephants that lived thousands of years ago are called—
   (A) bison
   (B) jungle dogs
   (C) mammoths
   (D) cattle

3. The bones in the story were found near—
   (A) a mountain
   (B) an ocean
   (C) a swimming pool
   (D) an apartment building

4. You can tell that mammoths—
   (A) were large animals
   (B) liked to swim
   (C) could fly
   (D) were tiny animals

5. The word "ages" in line nine means—
   (A) months
   (B) a few days
   (C) many years
   (D) several weeks

UNIT 40

Bridges are built for many reasons. Some bridges are built so that cars can cross over rivers. Others are made for trains to use. In the state of Washington, there is a very unusual bridge—it was built for squirrels!

The town of Longview has a very busy street. Many cars use it every day. Squirrels were being killed as they tried to cross the street. Mr. Peters built a bridge for the squirrels—one that would pass above the *traffic*. For years now, the squirrels have been able to cross safely from one side of the street to the other.

---

1. The best title is—
   (A) Bridges That Cross Rivers
   (B) How to Build a Bridge
   (C) A Bridge for Squirrels
   (D) A Very Busy Street

2. The story says that some bridges are used by—
   (A) swimmers (B) airplanes
   (C) trains (D) mice

3. Before the bridge was built, many squirrels were—
   (A) happy (B) killed
   (C) sick (D) tame

4. The story suggests that Mr. Peters—
   (A) hates children (B) is old
   (C) eats a lot (D) likes animals

5. The word "traffic" in line eight means—
   (A) clouds (B) state
   (C) deep river (D) moving cars

UNIT 41

Companies that sell food for dogs and cats test the food first. They find out what kind of food the animals like. They also learn what foods are good for pets. One company has a large house where they keep six hundred dogs and cats. The animals love living in the large house—they just eat and play.

Every day the animals are fed many kinds of food. An animal doctor watches to see what kinds they like. The doctor also finds out which foods help the animals stay healthy. The company can then sell the *finest* food for dogs and cats.

---

1. The best title is—
   (A) A House for Lost Animals
   (B) Testing Foods for Dogs and Cats
   (C) Why Meat Is Good for Animals
   (D) A Doctor Helps Sick Animals

2. The animals in the story live in a—
   (A) hospital (B) forest
   (C) large house (D) small room

3. The animals are fed—
   (A) nothing (B) once a week
   (C) very little food (D) many kinds of food

4. You can tell that dog food is—
   (A) sold in paper bags (B) tested for its taste
   (C) bad for dogs (D) never sold

5. The word "finest" in line nine means—
   (A) hardest (B) poorest
   (C) best (D) lost

UNIT 42

Every day, Chad Wilson rushes home from his third-grade class at school. He cannot wait to get back to his hobby—learning to use a special radio.

For hours, Chad listens to voices from around the world. He is not old enough yet to be allowed to *transmit* messages. But he can listen in as people talk to each other from near and far. "It will be a couple of years before I am allowed to send messages, but I'll be ready," Chad says. "I can't wait to get in touch with the people I've heard talk from Africa, Australia, and everywhere else."

---

1. The best title is—
   (A) Chad Wilson
   (B) Chad's Hobby
   (C) Life in Australia
   (D) Short-wave Radios

2. Chad is in—
   (A) second grade (B) fourth grade
   (C) third grade (D) fifth grade

3. With his special radio, Chad can—
   (A) write messages (B) do his homework
   (C) listen to messages (D) travel to Africa

4. You can tell that Chad is interested in people—
   (A) from other countries (B) with hobbies
   (C) his own age (D) who like music

5. The word "transmit" in line five means—
   (A) read (B) listen to
   (C) send out (D) collect

UNIT 43

In 1961, Charlayne Hunter-Gault became the first black woman to *attend* a college in Georgia. What she did helped change American history.

Today, however, Charlayne Hunter-Gault helps us keep track of history. For almost ten years, she was a newspaper reporter for the *New York Times*. She covered some of the most important stories about the black neighborhoods in New York. Now she works for a television news station. She can be seen almost every night on TV, helping people find out what goes on in their world.

---

1. The best title is—
   (A) The History of the *New York Times*
   (B) A College in Georgia
   (C) Charlayne Hunter-Gault: News Reporter
   (D) Famous Newswomen

2. Hunter-Gault studied at a college in—
   (A) New York
   (B) London
   (C) Georgia
   (D) Washington, D.C.

3. For ten years, Hunter-Gault worked for—
   (A) a college
   (B) a newspaper
   (C) her neighborhood
   (D) an oil company

4. You can tell that Hunter-Gault likes to—
   (A) teach history
   (B) report the news
   (C) take pictures
   (D) watch television

5. The word "attend" in line two means—
   (A) find
   (B) open
   (C) explain
   (D) go to

UNIT 44

It's fun to build castles of sand at the beach. Chandler had just come home from the hospital and had to stay in the house. He couldn't go to the beach to build a sand castle, so Chandler built a castle with cards.

It took Chandler eighteen hours to build the castle. He used seven thousand cards. When he finished, it was nine feet high. Chandler believes that it was the highest castle of cards ever made.

After all his friends had seen the castle, Chandler *swatted* it with a broom. Down it fell.

---

1. The best title is—
   (A) A Castle of Cards
   (B) Fun at the Beach
   (C) Chandler Gets Sick
   (D) Living in a Castle

2. The castle in the story was—
   (A) made of metal
   (B) made of wood
   (C) two feet high
   (D) nine feet high

3. Building the castle took—
   (A) five years
   (B) ten minutes
   (C) seven months
   (D) eighteen hours

4. Chandler couldn't go to the beach because he had been—
   (A) happy
   (B) sick
   (C) lost
   (D) busy

5. The word "swatted" in line eight means—
   (A) saw
   (B) learned
   (C) hit
   (D) ate

UNIT 45

An ambulance usually takes people to a hospital when they need immediate attention. Jean Stober drives an ambulance, but it doesn't carry *humans*. It carries animals!

Animals get sick and have accidents just like people. Many of them can be saved if they receive quick care. Stober gives them quick care. She is a good driver and can get to the animals fast. Before she puts the animal into the ambulance, Stober often gives it first aid. Then she rushes it to an animal doctor.

Jean Stober likes her work. She feels that animals should be helped just as people are.

---

1. The best title is—
   (A) Jean Stober and Her Ambulance for Animals
   (B) Quick Care Can Save People's Lives
   (C) Why People Like Animals
   (D) A Woman and Her Many Pets

2. The story says that Jean Stober is—
   (A) a pet-shop owner (B) an airplane pilot
   (C) a good driver (D) a good cook

3. Jean Stober rushes the animals to—
   (A) a farm (B) a circus
   (C) her house (D) an animal doctor

4. You can tell that Jean Stober—
   (A) cannot drive (B) likes animals
   (C) has a large family (D) can sing well

5. The word "humans" in line three means—
   (A) furniture (B) water
   (C) people (D) trucks

UNIT 46

Dick and his dog, Andy, were walking down the street. Dick heard a strange noise. Turning, he saw a huge bull running straight at them. Dick and Andy began to run. Then Dick tripped and fell!

The bull, which weighed over a thousand pounds, was nearly upon him. That's when Andy came to the rescue. The dog stood in front of Dick and began barking. Andy *yelped* so loudly that the bull stopped. This gave Dick enough time to get up and run away.

That night, Dick gave Andy a big steak for supper—instead of his usual dog food.

---

1. The best title is—
   (A) What Andy Likes to Eat
   (B) How Andy Saved Dick
   (C) A Nice Walk
   (D) A Pet Bull

2. When Dick saw the bull, he began to—
   (A) laugh (B) sing
   (C) fight (D) run

3. The bull in the story weighed—
   (A) 150 pounds (B) 600 pounds
   (C) over 1,000 pounds (D) less than 500 pounds

4. Andy was given a steak because he had—
   (A) been afraid (B) saved Dick
   (C) run away (D) kept quiet

5. The word "yelped" in line six means—
   (A) laughed (B) barked
   (C) hid (D) walked

UNIT 47

Trudy had a playhouse in the woods in back of her house. It had tables, chairs, a rug, and toy dishes. Every summer, Trudy and her family went on a vacation. While they were away, someone would go into her playhouse and steal the furniture and dishes. One summer, her mother did something to *safeguard* the playhouse.

Just before they went on vacation, Trudy's mother had a beekeeper come and put hundreds of bees in the playhouse. When they returned from their vacation, the beekeeper took the bees away. Nothing had been stolen. The bees had frightened the thieves away.

---

1. The best title is—
   (A) Trudy Buys a New Table
   (B) Bees Guard a Playhouse
   (C) Playing with Toy Dishes
   (D) Fun During the Summer

2. Trudy's playhouse was in—
   (A) her front yard
   (B) her bedroom
   (C) the woods
   (D) a park

3. The story says that the playhouse had—
   (A) beds
   (B) a stove
   (C) chairs
   (D) lamps

4. You can tell that the playhouse was—
   (A) ugly
   (B) not new
   (C) painted red
   (D) made of glass

5. The word "safeguard" in line five means—
   (A) protect
   (B) make
   (C) steal
   (D) paint

UNIT 48

Everyone knows that eggs break very easily. If one drops to the floor, it will break into many pieces. A class once had a contest. Each pupil was to pack an egg into a small box. Then the box was to be dropped from the top of the school building. If the egg didn't break, the pupil won a prize.

Some of the pupils put cotton around their eggs to protect them. Others used cloth or paper. Everyone thought that most of the eggs would be *smashed* anyway. Forty eggs were dropped from the top of the school. To the pupils' surprise, thirty of their eggs didn't break.

---

1. The best title is—
   (A) How to Cook Eggs
   (B) An Egg-dropping Contest
   (C) A Good Breakfast
   (D) A School Sells Eggs

2. The eggs were dropped from—
   (A) an airplane (B) a porch
   (C) the top of a school (D) a bird's nest

3. The story says that some of the eggs were protected with—
   (A) glass (B) wood
   (C) metal (D) cloth

4. You can tell that thirty of the pupils—
   (A) won a prize (B) were girls
   (C) didn't come to school (D) didn't like eating eggs

5. The word "smashed" in line eight means—
   (A) cooked (B) broken
   (C) laid (D) eaten

UNIT 49

Ted Joyce is an important person in Moreland, Massachusetts. He helps people with their taxes, checks out library books, and sees that the snow gets plowed and the roads get repaired.

It wasn't always like this. Moreland is so small that it could not afford to have someone run the town. Then Ted moved back after thirty years in the army.

Ted quickly offered to take over. He no longer had to work, so he didn't *require* money. The people of Moreland were glad to put him in charge. "I enjoy being a one-person office," Ted says. "You name it, I take care of it. Fun, isn't it?"

---

1. The best title is—
   (A) Ted Joyce: Army Man
   (B) Small Towns in America
   (C) Moreland's Master of Everything
   (D) How to Plow Snow and Repair Roads

2. Ted Joyce spent thirty years—
   (A) in Moreland
   (B) in the army
   (C) in the navy
   (D) as a police officer

3. Moreland is a small town in—
   (A) California
   (B) Maryland
   (C) Massachusetts
   (D) Wisconsin

4. You can tell that Ted Joyce—
   (A) doesn't do a good job
   (B) hopes to get rich
   (C) likes to help
   (D) is tall and thin

5. The word "require" in line eight means—
   (A) give
   (B) need
   (C) protect
   (D) say

UNIT 50

Did you ever hear of a goose that talks? Mrs. Boyko had one. Its name was Henry. It could say "grandpa," "I love you," "bad girl," and many other words.

Henry also liked to watch TV. When animals came on the screen, the goose became very excited. It even tried to talk to the animals. One thing Henry did not like was hats. If Mrs. Boyko wore a hat, the goose tried to *yank* it off her head.

Mrs. Boyko had Henry as a pet for a long time. Henry was part of the Boyko family for seventeen years.

---

1. The best title is—
   (A) Animal Movies on TV
   (B) A Pet Goose That Talked
   (C) How Long Animals Lived
   (D) A Trip to the Zoo

2. The story says that Henry liked to—
   (A) eat cake
   (B) read books
   (C) watch TV
   (D) sing songs

3. One thing that Henry did not like was—
   (A) shoes
   (B) hats
   (C) gloves
   (D) socks

4. The story suggests that Henry—
   (A) had no friends
   (B) could not walk
   (C) was an unusual goose
   (D) went to school

5. The word "yank" in line seven means—
   (A) show
   (B) pull
   (C) grow
   (D) wear

In Unit 44 you read about building sand and card castles. Now read about some buildings that were much harder to build.

There are ancient buildings in Egypt called pyramids. A pyramid has four sides that come to a point at the top. One is called the Great Pyramid. The Great Pyramid was built four thousand years ago. This pyramid was built for a king named Cheops. He is buried in the Great Pyramid.

The Great Pyramid is made of giant stone blocks. Each block is seven feet high. Many are eighteen feet across. They weigh as much as four thousand pounds each. People believe that there are over two million of these blocks in this giant pyramid.

How did the workers build this pyramid? They had no machines. They had no trucks. Each stone block was put onto a ship and carried up the Nile River. Hundreds of workers had to pull the blocks on sleds to the pyramid. It took many thousands of workers to build the pyramid.

A. Exercising Your Skill

Sometimes you learn things by "reading between the lines" of a story. Read the sentences below. On your paper, write each sentence that you think is probably true.

- Cheops was an important king.
- Building a pyramid was very hard work.
- Cheops made the pyramid himself.
- A pyramid took a very long time to build.

B. Expanding Your Skill

What facts in the story about the Great Pyramid helped you "read between the lines"? Write the sentence below on your paper. Under the sentence, write any facts that might help you know that this sentence is probably true.

Pyramids were important to the people of ancient Egypt.

C. Exploring Language

Read the paragraphs below. Think about how you would fill in the blanks. Then write the paragraphs on your paper with the blanks filled in. In some blanks you may use more than one word.

The Taj Mahal is one of the world's most famous buildings. It was built by an Indian ruler named Shah Jahan. This building in _____ was built by Shah Jahan for his wife. The ruler loved his wife very much. When she suddenly died, he was _____. He wanted to show his _____ for her. So he decided to build her the most beautiful _____ anyone had ever seen.

People came from all over the world to help with the Taj Mahal. More than twenty thousand workers _____ for eighteen years to build it. When it was finished, it was one of the _____ buildings in the world.

D. Expressing Yourself

Choose one of these things.

1. What do you think it would be like to help build a pyramid in ancient Egypt? Work with a partner and pretend that you are two of the workers. Tell each other how your day went—what you did and how you felt by supper time. Then act out your talk for your classmates.

2. How do you think Shah Jahan felt about the Taj Mahal? Imagine that you are listening to his words on the day when the building is finished. On your paper, write what you think he might say.